A Dream Come True

By Jordan Scrimshire

Illustrated by Taylor Miller

To my mother, Talitha,
and my Nana.

Thank you for selling everything
and buying the field
so that I could have the
Pearl of Great Price.

In the beginning, Father God, His son Jesus, and
Holy Spirit had a wonderful idea. Father God longed
for children, Jesus wished for a bride, and Holy Spirit
dreamt of a place to live. So together they decided to
make one body to be all of these things.

They crafted hands and eyes and ears and organs and arms and toes. Father God made each part look a special way to do a special task. The best part was that He designed each piece to fit together perfectly. It was a brilliant plan!

Jesus loved every part of the body even though it was not whole yet. He asked Holy Spirit to be their helper and live inside each piece. It was Holy Spirit's job to tell every body part where it needed to go and what it was made to do.

One day, Foot came to Father God and said, "I'm not a hand, so I'm not part of the body."

"No silly!" said Father God. "If you were a hand, how would my body be able to walk? You are so important to me! The body needs YOU. You have a gift to share."

Foot gave his daddy a big hug and ran off to meet his friends, Leg and Toe. Father God's kind words showed him that he was in the right place.

   Not long after, Ear sadly trotted over to Jesus and said, "I can't hear Holy Spirit tell me where to go. I must not have a place in the body."

   Jesus stooped down and looked lovingly at Ear. "You must wait a little longer," Jesus replied. "Holy Spirit wants to tell you where to go, but you must be patient. I have a special time for you to meet the part of the body that you will be closest to. Don't give up, my precious one. I am teaching you to hear my voice."

   A few days later, Ear found her place close to Eye and Mouth. Holy Spirit had shown her where to go just like Jesus promised.

Ear wasn't the only one that needed help though. Nose and Stomach were not getting along. Nose got angry and yelled at Stomach, "I don't need you!"

Immediately after the words came out, Nose began to feel sorry. Holy Spirit showed him that he was wrong.

"You need Stomach," Holy Spirit whispered.
"You may not see all the work he does, but he is
very strong and the body cannot eat or grow without
him. I love him just as much as I love you and both
of you are part of my body. You must learn to work
together, even when you disagree."

So Nose and Stomach decided that, even though
they didn't agree on everything, they could still love
each other because they were brothers. They both
decided that the body coming together was more
important than being right.

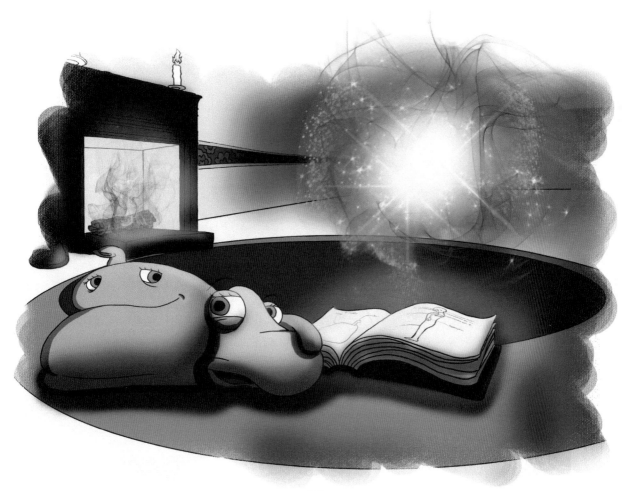

One day, Jesus noticed that the fingers were not speaking to other parts of the body.

"Fingers," Jesus said sadly, "You cannot be separated from the rest of my body."

"But Jesus!" said the fingers in unison, "they aren't like us! They don't look like us or think like us or talk like us."

"You're right!" agreed Jesus.

"Isn't it wonderful? You are all so unique! Father God chose a special place for you in this body. But the body won't work properly if everyone is not in their place. My bride is made up of more than just fingers," Jesus laughed. "You need the rest of the body too or you will not be complete."

Many of the fingers had not even realized that they had been excluding other parts of the body. However, after Jesus talked to them, they knew that their attitude and actions had to change. Even though it was difficult, the fingers split up and Holy Spirit showed each one it's rightful place in the body.

Holy Spirit lead every part of the body to its place. As they came together, it was easy to recognize the love of Father God that all of them carried. That love was what caused them to fit together perfectly, just as God had planned.

Joints and muscles formed between them and Jesus gave each part of the body strength to work as a team. Soon, they all began to move as one. God's magnificent dream was complete.

Jesus was the happiest He had ever been. His bride was ready! She was beautiful and radiating with glory because Holy Spirit had made His home inside of her. She was powerful and mighty and clothed in royal robes. She sat with Jesus on His throne, next to their daddy, Father God, where they ruled and reigned forever.

Lets Talk About That!

Did you know that YOU are part of the body of Christ? You are God's child, Jesus's bride, and a home for the Holy Spirit! God, Jesus, and Holy Spirit made you a special way to do a special task. You were made to fit together with other parts of the body. **You are God's dream!**

What part of the body do you think you are? An eye? An ear? A nose?

Have you ever felt like you weren't important, like Foot? What did Father God say to Foot? Go back to page 11 to find out.

God says the same thing to you! Without you, the body of Christ can't do what it was made to do. We might not feel important sometimes, but God sees everything we do. He is proud of you!

On page 13, Ear didn't know where she belonged. Have you ever felt like Ear?

Holy Spirit can help us! When Jesus was on the earth, He promised us that Holy Spirit would lead us into all truth (John 16:13). So, when you don't know what to do, ask Holy Spirit!

Nose said something mean to Stomach on page 15. Have you ever said something mean to someone, even though you love them?

Everyone is important in the body. Most people aren't just like you, but that's ok! Jesus made us all with different ideas and personalities, but we all need each other. We can still be in the same body, even if we don't agree on everything.

Have you and your friends ever left someone out like the fingers on page 16?

Sometimes when we have close friends, it seems like we don't need anyone else. But that's not true. How can we all work together if we only know people that are just like us? When we make friends with people that are different, we get to learn new things!

Dear Jesus,

Thank you for making me a special part of your plan. Thank you for loving me and giving me Holy Spirit to help me in everything I do. You are so wonderful!

Please help me to understand that you made everyone uniquely, and that's a good thing! Give us strength to work as a team so your dream can come true.

We love you, Jesus! Amen.

64743819R00015

Made in the USA
Charleston, SC
07 December 2016